salmonpoetry
*Celebrating 35 Years
of Literary Publishing*

The Language Hospital

JOHN MURPHY

(signature)

To Claire
with
Best wishes.

Published in 2016 by
Salmon Poetry
Cliffs of Moher, County Clare, Ireland
Website: www.salmonpoetry.com
Email: info@salmonpoetry.com

ISBN 978-1-910669-55-6

COVER IMAGE: Philomena Murphy.
Foreground (l to r): Mamie Casserly, Mary Jo Casserly (daughter of Mamie), Philomena Murphy
(daughter of Mary Jo), Louise Murphy (buggy, daughter of Philomena); Background: Katie Murphy
(daughter of Louise Murphy).
COVER DESIGN & BOOK TYPESETTING: *Siobhán Hutson*
Printed in Ireland by Sprint Print

Salmon Poetry gratefully acknowledges the support of
The Arts Council / An Chomhairle Ealaoín

For David, Louise, Stephen, and Katie

Acknowledgements

Thanks and acknowledgements are due to the editors, judges, and organisers of the following journals, anthologies, and competitions in which some of these poems have appeared:

Poetry Ireland Review: 'Bird, Lotus'

Cyphers: 'Akeldama,' 'Where The Brown River Flows,' 'Aurora,' 'Apollo'

The Moth: 'Stain'

Crannóg: 'Petronilla De Meath'

Even The Daybreak: 35 Years of Salmon Poetry: 'Iris and Hermes' [anthology]

Southword: 'Last Game Of The Night' [accepted for publication]

The FISH Prize 2013: 'Luminosity' [shortlist]

The iYeats Competition 2014: 'Minute By Minute They Change' [shortlist]

The Bridport Prize 2014: 'Nocturne' [shortlist]

The Strokestown International Poetry Prize 2015:
'The Nod' [Winner], 'Story [shortlist]

The UK National Poetry Prize 2015:
'Threnody Of The Campion Flowers For Paul Celan' [finalist]

The Bridport Prize 2016: 'Onions' [shortlist]

The Strokestown International Poetry Prize 2016:
'As If She Were Close' [Winner], 'Euclid And The Sunbird' [shortlist]

I am grateful to Aidan Murphy, Geraldine Mitchell, Colm Keegan, Joe Morris, Martyn Crucefix and Brian Kirk.

I am very grateful to the wonderful Jessie Lendennie and Siobhán Hutson for the immense work they do.

Finally, thanks to my family for their support and inspiration.

Contents

Bird

Do me a favour: shut up about your father.
Mine's twenty years dead, give or take
a week or two. And, no, I can't find my mother.
But I look for her. I do. Nights I walk

the borders of the past, listening for a one-note bird,
for the brassy claptrap of crows on the roof,
for a voice heard only in sleep, a word
in a dream. And when I sleep she speaks

through years long overgrown, through vines
that choke the light from one good day. It's July.
I'm eight years old. Neil Armstrong has yet to fluff his lines.
Look, she says, embracing a moon I'll never see again.

Her arms unfold like wings – she leaves too soon.
She leaves a trapped absence in the eaves of my room.

The Nod

Tonight the lights of new bungalows dance in the level water
    of the lake, and shadows from Jimmy the Hay's
shack and your grandparents' derelict house squat behind
    the wall of shoreline trees where Mick Casserly's boat
has collapsed in the bones of its timbers. For years now
    the fishing has been poor – the brown trout almost gone,
driven out, your cousin says, by pike introduced by coarsemen
    with no patience for fly-fishing and famine days
when every fly is the wrong fly and teasing rudd jump clear of
    the water, throwing sprays of diamonds off their backs.

The lake water is ice cold, the shock of it enough to stall
    the heart of a sick man, though when I was younger
I often swam in it, catching crayfish in a clear jar for our children,
    or wading out to watch voracious shrimp
feed among the reeds, and afterwards, drying off in minutes
    in the windless heat of an August afternoon.
I'll never swim again, never run as I once did at full tilt
    across an open field, unafraid of the limits
of my endurance, and I'll never again stand for profligate hours,
    mindless in the heaven of the passing world around me.

What was that world? A dust-lit kitchen twenty five years
    ago with a range and a wooden table on which
two pears touch, end to end, in a semblance of homely infinity;
    a bakelite telephone encrusted with peat
motes from the range where each night your grandmother
    heats iron blocks and wraps them in a blanket
to warm the bed we sleep in; a two-station TV to watch
    news and weather bulletins twice a day;
and the only comfortable chairs in the house, each side of
    the range: one for your grandfather, the other for guests.

A few months before he dies in his chair, Mick scrapes out
    his pipe and fills it — there is little or no talk
while the women are abroad in the town. Outside the window
    the lake is frosted silver by multitudes of small,
pointed waves; a crow on the roof coughs a raucous vowel.
    We settle down and for two hours no car passes;
the only sound is our breathing and a popping noise when Mick
    draws on his pipe. *Are you shaving yet?* is the sum of his talk.
I am twenty-six years old, a father myself, though to your grandfather
    I am still a child. *I am*, I answer, the remainder unsaid.

A postoffice van glides by on the road, breaching the air as if
    its engine were dead; the wireless,
turned low all morning, crackles a line from a sean-nós song;
    the fridge shivers in a vain attempt to keep
week-old milk from taint; tappets yammer in the back field
    where a tractor idles in neutral; the clock in the hall
ticks and chirps like a broken banjo; steps on the gravel;
    voices at the door; coming and going, a notion to go up
to the bedroom and look out at the lake field where the malt
    bull sleeps — five full minutes pass before he gives me the nod.

Euclid and the Sunbird

Keep Out, the sign says, but keeps out nothing
of the hawk that roves its half-mile eyeline
over the bent furrows and glinting shares
of a dragging horse that never sees the earth
it turns, plough-lined in guiding leathers.
And the bird's beating heart below its sight
ranges an eye, feeds the dropped line
a pulse that draws a shocking fall to pull
the morning down, and down, and down,
to six blind points of grip and concentration.
Keep Out, yet everything keeps in the moment
the talons hung on the rippling heat and held
the sky so suddenly open and alive that no air
could fill the lungs, and watching eyes, drawn
straight up on instinct to meet a bending line,
made a lambda of sparrow, hawk, and man.

Where The Brown River Flows

Here they come, the Friesians and Charolais,
   the Large Whites and Landraces, down
Oxmantown, down Aughrim Street,
Ross Street, Ashford and Arklow Street,
they run, the rivulets of dung turning
to rivers on Ben Eadair and Niall Street,
the crombied drovers calling and shouting,
their ash plants strafing polls and bleeding
haunches, fear and a strange exhilaration
everywhere on market day when children
crush in doorways and alcoves, well-used-to
but wary of the thundering hooves
   and the sudden grunt of diesel engines.
Here they come, the blessed of the country,
   the cattle ranchers and farmers, the dealers
and flush bucks in money-chocked boots.
Here they come, the spit-on-the-hand men,
the blowers and puffers, the gombeens
and sharps. They come and they come,
and beasts bellow in the slaughter races,
and ramps clang on the pavements,
and sticks jangle the grills and hollow rails,
and they turn in a ring of churning dust
where the auctioneer yammers the bids
and farmers pummel rosettes of money.
And still they come, they come until
   the blood drains from the killing floor,
the foundations drop, and Drumalee estate
slides over the cattle pens and abattoir,
the stench of crop and carcass lingering
for years —   And now they are gone,
one hundred and seventeen years of gore
and slaughter, a holocaust of beasts, ten
thousand hecatombs drained to the bones,
trotters and hooves, skulled, hung and cropped,

the slung curves of hooked meat
  cut clean as the torsos of mannequins.
They came and are gone, the cattle trucks,
  the glazed eyes that bulged between the slats.
The tanglers, drovers and penny boys gone.
The skull bolt and the brown river gone.
The greatcoats pressed, the boots polished,
the streets washed clean — all of it gone,
  everything put away or covered over.
This is civilisation. This is how it is.

Flights

Sometimes he waited for her to speak, but she wouldn't speak,
as if what she might say could wait, like the banked heat
of the fire he put down for the night,
until morning, when the sun like a vowel
opened the first sentence of the day,
and the flight he cancelled
would leave and return,
as he would leave and return in the shortening days;
and loading the washing machine
with yesterday's unrumpled, spotless sheets,
she would say, as she liked to say
when he returned from an evening walk,
a consonant of dark behind him in the street,
Put down that fire, love, before you go up.

Nocturne

I was moving from that house where,
forgetful, I kicked the milk bottles
down the front steps each morning.
This was the time after the other
place where space was a premium,
and my brother and I slept on
iron bunks in our parents' room.
In both places we heard much
we shouldn't have, and learned
firsthand the song of love's grief
from their night-burdened lips.
We never spoke of what was heard,
and what was heard we dispersed
as secrecy to our growing bodies.
At night now, in the place after
the last place (the second place),
bits of music come tunnelling back,
loose casts of what was heard before:
the husk words of a song adrift
in the breathless dark; the lost air
of a passage of minims driven in bone.

A Different Snow

Like Tu Fu you know the sky and river
know nothing of hours made years,
or the pity of your lost friend.

Still, I imagine both of you meeting again,
on a corner of Dame street,

under a mural of two men embracing.

Or on the crowded steps of a bar at closing time,
having glanced each other in the crush.

Or better still by the lake in Stephen's Green,
under falling cherry blossom,

                    a different snow —

But this is what happens on a bright June day.

You've chained your bike to a fleur-de-lis railing,
around you is a Victorian square.

She looks away — just as you notice her,

        just as you say hello.

For minutes you stand in the range of her breath,
erasing decades.

    She speaks over you, laughs

when you laugh, your voices young again —

In silk slippers she walks away, wheeling her step-through.

The woman whose husband was once your friend.

Who doesn't turn or wave.

Whose only question was:

Where do you live now?

Verbotene Musik

It's dark. There's no light save the moon.
His small deft fingers work the mesh,
inches at a time. Already, he knows the tune,
the notes leaping clear from the crush
of staved pages he draws through the lattice —
he bites his tongue, mustn't sing — nothing quells
the sacred music in his head. His conscience is ice.
These pages are my food and drink, he tells

himself, his brow sweating, his small hands dry.
He prays, *Let Johann Christoph sleep tonight*.
Later, transcribing a sheet he will never play
in a room where the moon is not his only light,
he learns a purer disobedience, closes his eyes,
masters the sound of his God's disguise.

Aurora

It's half past three and the veteran birds
are singing their complicated songs.
They don't know why they are singing
to a starless dawn, or why we sailed from Olympus
to Valhalla in a bireme of sinking dreams.
On broken thwarts we rowed all night,
skirting the edge of a green horizon —
the one that will one day drop us off for good.

On the other side of the world,
blurred on a bed of coloured stones,
two goldfish wake in a glassy algal mist.
In the armour of their golden scales
they cower behind a palisade of plastic grass,
hiding from the moon and the sun.
They don't know there is nothing to be afraid of —
nothing, but the sudden meaninglessness of love.

Once I Was Beautiful

Sometimes as the years piled on, she wondered:
Am I the only one of my friends, my workmates,
my family, who knows I am a corpse marching
to ashes and dust in a churchyard, a crematorium?

I'm no smarter or better than any of them,
and no matter the greatness of the books I read,
or the learning I profess, the small glories
I have won in a world half-drowned in fame,

infamy, and the blood of wretches far away,
are less than nothing. My youth was heartless,
a doll crawled too close to a greenwood fire.
It sputtered and went out, yet what remains

is a rarity of wisps in the heavy air,
and these few faint aromas are sweetest of all.

For Living Things Are Revived By Food, And Clocks, By Lapse Of Time, Become Slower, Never Faster

Let us savour our sprung minutes of verge and foliot,
    stackfreed and hammered coil, all of unclustered
    time brass-burst
in mechanisms prone to damp, rust, dust, weakening
    because it is an inanimate thing subject to great stress.
    And where would we be
were it not for Alexander's war machines, sprung beams,
    starved women's plaits, sinew skeins, the windlass gear
    that spared the Macedonian
arms at Tyre, miniaturised in the first fusees? Remembering,
    too, the clock smugglers: A great number of rascals
    and pedlars and juellers, who brought
divers merchandise unacustomed, all under the colour
    of the Trussery of the ambassadours.
    Nor should we forget Dallam's organ clock,

gifted by Elizabeth to the Sultan for safe passage of
    the English fleet. Four times a day it played
    with majestic stiffness and jigged
its racks of dancing automata: In the tope of the orgon, being
    16 foute hie, did stande a holly bushe full of black
    birds and thrushis, which at the end
of the musick did singe and shake their wynges. Dallam
    kept his head and cranked out his repertoire of
    Elizabethan tunes: And suche thinge
as I coulde until the cloke strucke, and then boued my
    head as low as I coulde, and wente from him
    with my backe towardes him. Which brings us
to Parliament and the Astronomer Royal who welched on
    the untrained master carpenter, Harrison, denying him
    his deserved prize for three decades

spent perfecting his clock, a sea-going masterpiece with a
    rate undreamt of by Leibniz, Newton, Halley,
    Huygens, or Hooke: . . . If it so please
Almighty God, to continue my life and health a little longer,
    they the Professors (or Priests) shall not hinder
    me of my pleasure,
as from my last drawing, viz, of bringing my watch to a
    second in a fortnight . . . And so, as I do not now
    mind the money (as not having occasion
to do so, and withal as being weary of that) the Devil may
    take the priests . . . We praise and glorify him,
    our patron saint of accuracy,
and with him Larcum Kendall, whose Harrison replicas
    navigated Cooke to Antarctica, and Bligh to Pitcairn
    and an infamous mutiny.

And lastly, before we rise, let us praise and remember
    one John Arnold, inventor of a mode of
    escapement of such a nature that friction is utterly
excluded from it; and in consequence, the use of oil,
    that bane to equality of motion, is rendered wholly
    unnecessary: and whether the material be
a diamond, steel, brass, or piece of wood, is perfectly
    indifferent, as they are all equally proper for the
    purpose. And whatever our measured moments
may or may not be, let us say amen to the fact that we can
    dally here at liberty, contemplating scaled shadows
    and strontium clocks rated to one second in five
billion years, oblivious to the lash of time quirting through
    the pulsing bacilli of a bedside radio clock,
    without escapement, stackfreed, or fusee.

Time And Life

When my mother's number is called
the doctor takes her firmly by the arm,
and tells me: *Wait here, young man.*
Read a magazine. She'll not be long.

I whistle through photo stories
of Hell's Angels in Los Angeles,
Broadway's gamine starlets,
the Tet Offensive underway.

A lurid centrefold gives me pause —
GIs flaming a hut between
ads for Florida homes —
twin staples in a crease of smoke.

Shuffling wrappers and biro tops,
I empty sweetshop histories
from sticky pockets, daydream
invisible armies on the move.

But the sanitised air is suddenly warm,
and all at once I feel her absence
everywhere. And when she slips out
the door of here and all harm, I wonder

what happens in that inner sanctum
where the sudden movement of life
is a newsreel reversed, and the thin reed
of my body swallows ungovernable fire.

Cranmer And The Yellow Flower

I can't get excited about waterways or rivers,
poorly shod horses or whores. I'm tired of allures
and talk of jonquils and roses, modes of romance
in churches whose lights are not prayers.

But the flower below the great hedge,
with its dead head of crushed yellow petals,
makes a gesture I can call pitiful,
bowed as it is to its own shadow.

It says nothing. But could it laugh,
it would laugh with bemusement
at whatever has come to my mind.
Something about a storm of roses.

If this yellow flower could speak to me
there would be no conversation,
no rose storm in a weather of language,
only suspicion, mutual and unfathomable.

The storm of roses on my mind speaks
a plain garden whence it came, climbs
through the holes of a mask, eyes both
ways blindly. But here in the King's garden

a kestrel plummets over the great hedge.
When it misses a bird whose name
I have forgotten, it comes to mind
I am sad I came this way so sorrily.

Midwintering

There was light enough on that cold
and drowning day, but no shaft of gold lit
our stumbling passageway of holy streets and
lanes. We knew it all and brooked no kyrie eleison
or klaxon warning call. On forgotten roads we abandoned
everything we loved and spiked the past with the flags of our
convenient histories. We threw our loaded dice against the stars
and played games with glorious mysteries. Our luck ran out in a thousand
bars. From ordinary liaisons in ordinary time we escaped the drunk
tank of reason, and then broke in again to our accepted season,
naked and sublime. No downpour washed our guilt away,
but a thin light sang like a crucifix in the wind when we
stormed the breach of God's dark mind, kept our
sunlit selves, left our madness behind.

Iris and Hermes

And our special powers? Winged feet
to patrol the shifting borders,
the contested zones of occupation,
flimsy aces lashed to our ankles,
ligaments of luck and kilter fluttering
below the sheets in a valley running
south of the neutral zone — here, a lifetime's
worth of weights and measures sweats.

Back to back, all things being equal,
a sort of river commerce flourishes
between us — nothing so glib or slick
as double entry, contracts for difference
or gilt returns, just a night trade of rounding
errors, hedged bets, and devaluations,
the arbitrage of psychopomps,
the reinvention of fire.

Little Boy Blue

How bright the room, how blue
the blanket with the red stain
that swaddled you, how blue
the eyes that first beheld you.

When you were born you looked at
your mother and smiled. You never
took another breath, closed your eyes,
and darkened the house to sleep forever.

The Planxty Tree

My leitmotif is a music of branches, the resinous
phrase she made when she was the quicken tree.
This was before the burning, the burning she suffered
for me. In every town I sing of her quickening and how
she came to be. I took my calling from a harpist who
was two parts sky, one part sea. He showed me the way
to limber the planxty. The beginning an intimation of
the west wind, the centre a green and frothless wave,
the end the airy lee of a barren island, praising arrival
where nothing has gone before. My rowan grows restive
at night. She chambers a breeze and sets her sisters dancing.
In the curve of my agile hand she fashions a sail. All night
we circle the barren islands, singing, praising. All night
the green waves lift us and the rock samphire glows.

Yet at first light she'll tap my eyelids, that fecund knock,
her sisters, the Hazel, the Willow, and the Yew, ever awake.
And when the fire blazes I'll birth the raw tune, remembering
the day I felled her with her dancing sisters and made the harp.
Saint Brigid's Day. The low sun behind them, their branches
burning. My eyes blind as the rowanberries in the frost.

Odds

1

This place will soon be a university, but once
it was a seventy acre asylum, a facility where

abject men filed out to an airless playing field
for daily exercise, and though I can't remember

how many laps they made, their shuffling gait
and faltering steps have stayed with me,

the distraction of them enough to interrupt
day-long ball games in the moss-stained alley

they circled before returning to rooms where bare
bulbs glowed on all but the longest days of summer.

And I admit we were often afraid, though not because
of the men – they never harmed us – wary

as we were of the mischievous rumours
of money offered for favours in the bushes.

2

I didn't believe the rumours – the men were fearful,
and there was a palpable mystery

in their fear. What kept them in line as they walked
around the pitch oblivious to us and the sensations

of the world around them, obedient in their crumpled
neatness? Heads down they traipsed behind

a blocky warden, and while we stared, we never made
jokes or laughed at them, never heard them speak,

never spoke a word to them, absorbed as we were
in our common ignorance, thinking them lunatics;

and in so far as we understood their lives,
we witnessed their loneliness, a falling away

of something human in their silence, and knew this kind
of life was a possibility, however remote, for some of us.

3

We paid no heed to most of the trouble coming
and going as the nights wore down to shouts

and flagons breaking on the Richmond boundary wall;
heroin was a thin black line on the horizon, but Dublin

was still a mood and a breeze, and we would go home
in ones and twos, never worrying about safety in numbers,

taking the short, uncovered punt between
the darkening pitches to the Cabra gate,

the North Circular Road, and Hanlon's corner,
hoping we'd avoid the gangs of Annamoe, and the boys

we feared the most: a mouthy knifeman whose glassy skin
and blonde curls reminded me of Alexander the Great;

and his sidekick, a hefty psycho less articulate
than the Alsatian cross he unleashed with a huss.

4

A mood and a breeze — or so it seemed,
and still seems, a poem rising from the ruined

architecture of a dream. None of it exists, yet nothing
was more real than a shakedown on the street

for odds in broad daylight; or a punch in the face
from a sovereigned fist; or the light like bleached sheets

behind the infirmary outhouses, and you and me going home,
our palms fat from hours of handball, meeting on the narrow path

the two of them coming towards us with the slope-backed dog.
There was no place to run or hide in the open trap

we'd walked into. I was frightened, more frightened
than you were, but as they closed on us some protective

instinct tempered me, and what could I do
but veer us off the path to draw their intent.

5

When they followed us out into the field,
I hid my stripling fear and told you to stay behind

me no matter the stakes, aware at the same time
that my body understood what was happening

in a way my coward's mind would never know,
fear lifting the hair on the back of my head,

and there was no more to be said, no discussion,
no answering back, only the approaching

humiliation and debasement of a random beating.
Ten feet away from us they shouted the odds,

slapping their fists, the dog straining and jerking
the leash, but when they were close enough

my fist drew back and dropped the blonde boy
with a haymaker that flattened his manly nose.

6

Through an urge to retch I heard myself speaking
with someone else's voice, asking the stunned muscle

if he wanted the same, the dog yipping and snarling,
smelling the wrong blood, his gawping master

dismayed and awry, grunting and hussing,
too late, the enraged mutt bamboozled,

his misfiring instinct turning him back
on his leashman's arm, which made us laugh;

and even as we circled them they hadn't the wit
to press the odds, must have known nothing

about simple possibility and probability,
because they could have murdered us

on that darkening acre, but we were going past them now,
into longer shadows and the humid scent of bluebells.

Luminosity

Remember this: you're one of us, he says,
when you turn at the door. His dark eyes
shine with the immense density of a wasp's.
The sun rises. A one-riff rooster blares morning.

Needing answers you stand on a rotten lock gate,
looking down at a gravel-eyed stranger in green water.
All afternoon he watches you fish from a bag
of chandlers, white handfuls of live questions.

Late in the evening ice cubes rattle
like quartz in your glass. New Year's Day
is dressed in a lint of snow. In a spirit
of renewal you give up loose change.

On the long way home the moon
shivers in a cloud like a conjuror's bird.
Drenched elver heads slope by in rain-sleeked hoods.
Motorway lights curve and flow like melted candy.

This is what Noah would have seen
had the flood's last contraction washed up
this transience: a herring crush of humanity
in the beak of a guzzling clock; a night

when your old man's eyes are timed to brighten
with child-like luminosity. *How do you do?* he asks.
Who let you in? Unsaid, undone, the years press in.
Who are you? he asks. *Tell me again.*

Petronilla de Meath

The flaying seconds go, as all time goes,
and going slowly on, the inches and miles go,
and so the journey to my dying goes,
slow, and hard, and halt, its length and time go.

And the inch of time builds in the slow miles
I have walked for days, whipped and flayed
through six godly parishes to a kindling where
the living fire is mine, and the seconds candling

my hot breath burn centuries down inches
of miles to my confession. Three ways I burn
yet still I live, and my brightness goes down
in second, breath, and inch, into Lord Ossory's fire

to meet, like Shadrach, Meshach, and Abednego,
Death, the fourth and last, the king of fire.

Terminals

He stands to, and faces himself again,
as one more morning's features mark
a day present, and the white-edged sun,
perfect as a pill, rolls free on cue from the dark,

its sharp, medicinal light more bitter
now than battery terminals to the tongue
he once babbled in his boyhood's mouth.
Man after man, man after boy, a long

line of them forms neatly behind him:
boy after child, child after infant, newborn infant —
but in front, older men close up, their faces
invisible tomorrows, whose last instant

is the approaching murmur of a summer
that seemed as though it might never end.
So many graves behind and before a man who,
with little means, obeys the common command

of the gods who rarely speak to him,
to befriend time's ghosts, and in that befriending
lay them, hour by hour, on the grave of days
to an end that never meets its ending.

As If She Were Close

My mother is chasing me. All over the house.
No, this is not a nightmare. It happened,
thirty or so years ago. She is waving an
empty cigarette packet I'd neatly opened
to expose a writing surface. This is where
I wrote my first poem. A knot of gritty phrases
about a battle in Vietnam or Iwo Jima.
I can't remember where, but I'd dropped it
or thrown it away and forgotten about it:
my spider pencil crawl of a treatment.
A Sunday afternooner, a black and whiter.
The kind my mother liked, as long as Garfield
or Cagney starred. But my poem has no stars.
Just a bloodless jungle of men killing each other
in childish, thrilling ways. She finally catches
me, arms crossed like a corpse under her bed.
John! It's very good! You wrote a poem!

I'm seven or eight years old, and I know
whatever the thing I've done, it has a power
to frighten, a frightening power. One to shunt
aside until years after she's dead. Where I find
myself in the departure lounge at Heathrow,
waiting to connect as my American bosses say.
My slim ticket ready in my hand, and hours
to kill before boarding. And it begins again.
A full thirty years since I nipped it in the bud.
As if she were close. I'm writing a poem about
my mother in the space on the back of the card.
Something very simple about us walking along
the quays on the long way home from the auction
she used to love. It's straightforward, honest, plain.
But there's a powerful feeling, too. Like my heart
is physically moving to the wrong side of my chest
where it should not be. And the bloody thing makes
me cry. God damn it, but I can't stop writing it now.
I keep going on with it, on and on. What else can I do?

Sandymount

She brooched him with a memory, a sunny
look that pricked his skin and shrank him
to an atom of himself in the burning
glass of her long forgetting gaze.

Now he remembers the million lights on water
still twinkling there, and deaf to a silence
that pursues him everywhere, he talks loudly
to all who'll listen, telling all but his grief.

Words are redundant in that old story
where only a smudge labours the page,
a glyph of loss — himself — under
the grey smoke of the chimney stacks.

Here is shade and silence, a solid grief, too,
but a requiem pours from a car radio,
and the sand of a reckless score of years
runs through his eyes and ears.

Time works its violence, fills every gap
with glittering rubbish. He saw it, once,
in living technicolor, the murderer
behind the monochrome before his eyes.

Augustine On The Beach

Must I tell you again how the wind blows
emptiness through my too-full head,
how the sea cools the fire of exhausting passion,
how abstinence has lodged in me the fashion
of a famine, and every memory is indigestible bread?

Or should I walk again on that windless beach
where not a grain of sand stirred and waves
made no sound, where ships cleaved distances
of inches in whole afternoons, and our chances
ran after us then away from us into the sea caves?

There is more of you now in your going,
and more of me in the absence you hold of me
than the half-man who braces himself in a breeze
that blows away, for good or ill, all that froze
in him the remembrance of quiet seas.

And if I am less than I ever was, you become more
than you ever were to a mind honed on dilemmas
of blunting soul and flesh, going but not gone
until you are proved nowhere, and yet you are one
with everywhere, proof of difference and sameness.

Prayer

A kneeling shadow I sometimes shelter in;
a placeless table with four empty chairs;
and through the french doors, the grey light
of a town garden whose one climbing rose
I uprooted mid-summer and tore from a wall.

Here are plumped cushions; a blue suite;
the jade glass lid of an Italian desk;
a lingering must of artisan candles;
posh jackets in a closet you could sleep in:
the guff and no trousers of a bachelor life —

That night in Dublin, I walked home
under the trees in rain that hung beads
of starlight on the branches.
A bird fell singing through the dark,
a song that took from us the rest of the road.

I searched the ditches, but all I found
was a feather and a bone whistle.
The wind blew a cadenza, and blown beads
silvered the verge. Millions of white bells
opened their mouths in the river —

Somewhere my children wait for me,
as I wait for them, with a welcome
as fresh as the broad lowland rain
that washes through me when I say
the words of a prayer we used to say.

If A Lion Could Talk

"Of course I talk, but mostly I listen
    for sick beast noises on the great plains,
and my voice, when I speak, is the wide open
    echo of bones I powdered to dust.
In the evening, washes of blood fill the sky
    and the light falls away for what might
be forever under the immense fleece of night.
    And when my night belly growls, a roar leaves
the chamber of my ribs like a god's curse
    blasted from a temple to percuss and shake
the world. The million-hooved stampede
    will answer me, and the hyena gangs
will yip and trespass wherever I lead,
    which is always and ever the same places.
In dry river time I dream of marrowbones
    and the meaty neck of my greatest joy,
a buffalo who runs with four lions on his back.
    I treasure no memory but the one where I fought
my father in the valley of tusks where
    elephants go to die. We met each other
as two storms colliding, and I was for the first time
    the power of my full-grown mane. I took the load
of his fire and wind into my head when I killed him
    with a river-spanning bite and drank his blood.
Afterwards, I went on quiet pads to the river
    where the tall ones live among the slender cattle.
There was singing, drumming, feasting, a smoking fire.
    I watched the succulent dancers, and suffered
the racket they made until two spearless elders
    wandered in reach of my favourite claw.
Both men were drunk and unaware, and one of them spoke:
    (I translate roughly), *Good to feast. Good to drink.*
Better to fuck a virgin bride. Better yet to murder an enemy.
    Better still to lie under the stars and sleep peacefully —

Close by I heard a hyena snuffle in the chest cavity
    of a gazelle, and the river cattle lapping their fill.
A mantis cloud gripped the moon. The bush grew quiet —
    and then, as I moved closer, the other one said:
The best of all is never to have been born. All as true, I thought,
    as killing dark followed hungry light, but the last? —
I didn't understand what I could not wish or say."

Tarantella

The webs are white with dew
on the swings, and the rose is dead.
Long transparent legs trail lines of silk
from galled branches to the potting shed:
Pholcus is hunting for *Teganaria* stew.

She fears no other spider, not the wolf,
or the orb-weaver; even the fighter
Drassodes, the foot-trapper, is a milk
and honey snack for this leg biter
and husband eater. She's a skinny scruff

whose pad's a mess, an improviser who
shuns the baroque of traditional webs. Her skewed
lines are more Charlie Parker than Acker Bilk,
and she never bothers with fads like glue.
With legs like hers, would you?

Pimp

When I open the mirrored doors to touch
the rack of clothes you left behind,
I'll give them sinews and muscles,
a body, arms, legs, a one-track mind

that isn't theirs, and send them packing
down the steps to the hall, out the door,
where they'll march the sorry length of a street
until, empty again, they come begging back for more.

Akeldama

The fox climbs down from the station wall
and crosses the street in twilight,
ducks in and out of manicured hedges,
a thread of russet working dense privet —
And beyond the well-tended gardens,
thousands labour in the city where solid
plumes tint the pristine sky, but no siren
sounds the end of the working day —
And I am reliably informed these wind-break
palms are New Zealand Cabbage Trees;
though I've always known the transformations
and filtrations of twilight on this vivid coast
are without limit. Number overlords us more
than we think, naturally, continuously,
and never has the multitude of stars in the arc
of this twinkling bay been the same
on consecutive nights. Somewhere,
someone wants to know how many times
Judas counted his borrowed silver,
asking if they were shekels or staters —
And a man in a mackintosh is taking countless
photographs of the city and its people,
the first greens of the river, its glittering
midnight offices and plain dawn rosaries.
In a monochrome snap, my mother
smiles like a younger Judy Garland,
the river and city composed behind her,
colour leaching into grey surfaces,
light coming from every pore of her face —
There she is — but into what future is she going?
What is the gross acreage of that potter's field?
And how many times will I allow
the phone to ring before answering?
Now I am abandoning my desk, driving,
to a hospital, too late, finding her
already dead, and not even the marks
of resuscitation spoil her lovely face.

Borders

A green tear glistens on the mountain side,
and gulls shriek above a slant of river.
Fumes lace the air.
   A harpist murders Bach.
      All under a sun as warm as a rotten apricot.
         This is the saddest place on earth, she says,
and she knows better than most, having lived
through a siege.
         *Even your mountains and rivers
are permanently soused*, she goes on, as if
they were mine.
         To exist they have to be.
Across the valley wet furrows gleam,
and lush clouds shade the daytime moon
but can't conceal its droop of grinning scars.
Boys and girls with heads like stones drift from
a parish game, some of them wrapped in the flag
of a disputed nation.
         If we stay here we'll die of thirst, she says,
and the mountain falls in the arms of the laughing river.

Threnody Of The Campion Flowers
For Paul Celan

Far-off threnody, you are a liquid command to a me,
listener inactively.
     Your oar vestiges thread waters none
and no one walks for lack of faith,
and the near docks

plagued by clouds flash redly below the timber pilings.

Far-off threnody, you lament a he that cannot sing
without the him that makes him half a whole again,

the place of burial where none and no one finds a self,
the unfinishable image of death.

Threnody, your deep oar stroke pulls a lock of water,
opens a wave over the fish pulse where hope
lives in stone shallows.

In your hollow stands an almond where stands nothing
of oar vestiges and the marked songs of water,

of deepest water where low clouds cannot swim
or redly flash an ion sea.

The ion nothing stands where nothing is the king of almonds,
and the almoner summons a threnody

whose vestiges mark the fingerless waves

with the ring of death.

Far-off threnody, you refrain almonds to a king,

to one who walks upside down on clouds
tinged with dugouts of blood,

the sundered edges of grave pilings.

Came, came a song, you came as a threnody over deep waters
and your oar vestiges thread the living roots of souls

through eye-prayers of nothing and no one
and none.

Came as a threnody when the pilings sank in annihilations of light
as no salvation, sank softly under the threads of a brighter sun

and the incoming waves of the campion flowers
in verses of gorse-light.

Milan

When she returns, nothing stirs in the room
where his work is strewn about. Not even
the wind-up bird, last of seven, whose key
is stuck, whose mechanical eye yet gives
her his iron look of love. Nothing moves
but her hand opening the most dangerous,
calf-bound book — the one she loves least,
never finished. She waits. A faint drumming —
The chirr of wings — Louder and louder,
it swells to a hurricano of flying volumes,
all of them singing at once, his canticles
and hymns, madrigals and ballads, oceans
of dust making her retch. Her human noise
frightens the spirits, and a sprite who cowers
behind the drape, who stole the still wet page
he thinks she came for — half-drowned men,
the conspiring wave in pearl and crimson,
night birds shrieking counterfeit doom —
When she traces the invisible signature
in air, the books fall down around her feet,
shut themselves. Need never be opened again.

Apollo

i.m. Michael Murray

He threw his discus and harled his scores
of years with a handful of summer air.
Where he rose up, a blue sun
froze him trembling there.

Sixty summers come and go.
The eye of a crow-glazed lake outstares
the solitary evening star.
A gas lamp mantle glows with sleepless fire.

Let him shine in his armature of stars.
Let no price of heaven be exacted.
Let it be written in the book of souls
that he was love with all the guff subtracted.

Onions

My dad is eating raw onions, big as apples.
He's eating the onions while cooking a fry
in the black pan. I'm angry but frightened.
I tell him what I think of him. My mother
and sisters are in the other room, listening.

Dad doesn't turn around. What he's mumbling
I can't quite say. There was a farm at the end
of our garden, past the dead cherry blossom
choked by a diesel spill. Always in Spring we
couldn't sleep with the racket the lambs made.

Do you hear me? Dad mutters, cupping my neck.
You're nothing. You know that? Nothing. What?
In the year that I've outgrown him, he goes
too far. I lift him off his feet, want to hurt him.
I get in his face. So I'm nothing? Am I? What?

There's a silvery rustling behind the freezer.
Foil bottle caps I'd dropped to catch a mouse.
But I'm not here to shine my torch in the dark.
In the lightless bottoms where the motor growls,
something hesitates then scuttles away.

I'm there in the kitchen light of that Spring
evening, waiting until there's nothing
left to say. I'm holding him in the silence
he was born to give me. Stranger to myself,
I unclose my fist, let him go.

Minute By Minute They Change

A broad street where choking dust
swirls around a singing girl;
a galleon-headed horse nosing
oats on a footpath that was once
the route of a wayfaring saint:
and all else in the offing for a town
that knows nothing of what will come,
the plan laid in the numbered days
of uniformed men wavering like
grass behind a wall that in hours
will break and crumble like wet slate.
Mingled with the singing, the clop
of hooves, the banter of strangers —
who years later will remember,
in the given names of streets, lanes,
and burning corners, the names of men
they never knew — is an exhalation,
an implacable disturbance of air.
The soldiers' faces turn to vapour,
their limber muscles to soft rain;
and in the butcher's shop the tiled
face of a bull runs blood and grease
to a killing floor — the whistle blows,
and history crawls into a smoking ruin,
into hearts at anchor like a massed fleet.

Substitute

The saccharine words of the candy floss song
sugar the lips that never touched the lips.
And the hands, under the vamping hands that never
met the hands, second-guess the fingertips.

Stag

Whole and human I watched you bathe,
heart-stunned to a momentary silence,
but when I cried out to my friends
your wrath came down on me
with a malevolence that shattered
the bones of my skull. I couldn't keep
schtum. I'd have fucked you there
and then, but your rip and pull invaded
the dogs and I couldn't turn or run.
Corus and Charops tore my flank,
Arethusa and the rest fought neck-deep
in the flub. They didn't know me, Artemis,
but I knew myself, and the inverted thoughts
that burst through my skull – desire and ecstasy –
were the blunt, dead ends of the best of me.

Lotus

No one knows you. And you know no one.
Not even your children. But life and history
are lived one day at a time, and rather than lie alone
on your bed with an unlit cigarette, go to your children,
tell them a story, someone else's, or one
that comes to you like a long forgotten song
your mother sang, days before you were born.
Speak, read a few pages, learn to listen
for the sound of children listening, and soon
it will be too dark to read and you will go alone
into a trust you have been given with words
that are more than spaced silences.
No one knows you, but if they listen to you,
tell them a story. It doesn't matter if it's true.

Vrelo Bosne

For days the untouched banquet lies stale at your feet,
and the year thickens like swill in a trough. Pride weighs
the pearl of price through which you see everything,
and plunging waters sluice the gold from yesterday.

Don't talk to me about charity or kindness,
or the simplicity of love. Don't ask me to tell you
where the blue gentian grows, or to pronounce
in a filial way the name of this whirlpool —

I remember only the cemetery, the prayers we said
at your young father's grave, how you weighed clouds
in your hands, rocked to holy words I didn't understand.
In your mother's house strangers cast lots for your clothes.

The Language Hospital

Open to all weather, there are no walls,
only the stretched rubble of peoples
and places, fragments of glass, timber
and bone, everything fragile, mutable.
The aisles are empty. There are no physicians,
no cures, only the embalming residues
of dust — the razed buildings of Gaza,
Stalingrad and Troy. Perpetually dying
they live in perpetual resurrection,
witnessing through coinless eyes all
but the sign: *Do Not Resuscitate*.
Visitors are discouraged, though some
venture to save, in the final moment,
a word from the frictive kiss of a grave.
Admissions are attended, but nothing stirs
except a breath that blows through a tree hung
with silver coins, its one good root cleaved
to the earth. And when the breath turns,
a word echoes through the remains
of siege engines — onager, mangonel,
ballista, trebuchet — hair bales
and razor wire, gas canisters, morphine
vials, rocket launchers, drones, cartoons,
a stone child, pantheons of gods, rows
of unmarked graves, the airless lungs
of ghosts where synonyms of love and hate
skim the abyss until, answerless, the breath
gives up the word to the poem held in the glance
between the child and the Medusa, and nothing is lost.

Meiteamorfóis

Her outstretched fingers barely span my palm. Her curls, when washe
    fall down to her heels. She is dancing a reel the length
of the room, steps invented in the moment, for the small
    occasion of bedtime, the presence of grandparents,
the sheer heaven of it, her feet patterning a phrase a foot
    from ground without music, just a steady displacement
of light and air, as if she had stopped moving, as if only the floor,
    the room, and the whole house were moving,
framing her above the carpet she has blurred to a primal pattern,
    the gist of movement, and all of us caught
in the wild performance, becoming light ourselves, our souls
    moving sideways, one through the other.

Who taught her to dance like this? Who taught us to clap
    in time as if our lives depended on it?
Her thin legs scroll sentences in a language without names.
    She steps through us, bringing us one through
the other, the dance unrepeatable, and never again
    will her virtuoso footfall arrest time and form
as it does now. But she is tiring and we are backsliding
    to a dimension where human magic has no place
in passing seconds, where we are displaced as strangers
    to ourselves. She takes her bow and leaves
the stage. The room bobs to a halt. Tables and chairs precipitate
    to form. One from another, we are separate.

Separate like my schoolboy face and Miss Hanvey's hand,
    when she says: *Tae*, and misconstruing, I answer, *Tae*,
echoing, not translating as the lesson demands, a gout of air
    rushing to and away from my face when her hand
bounces a slap that resonates around the room, through the legs
    of rusting desks, pinging the icy radiators,

catching the stiff globe where a child's inky handprint covers
    half of Africa, a thumbprint just north of Biafra
and — I swear to God — creaks it half a revolution to Australia,
    where uncle Tommy lived after Anzio
and demob to Canada — *Siúcra, subh, im : say them in English!*
    she says, hand poised, *As Béarla! As Béarla! As Béarla!*

The words are not my words, and the words are not
    the teacher's words, nor the teacher's teacher's
words, nor for that matter my father's words, teaching me
    the soul of a name is death, that when I fail to protect
my brother on the street, I am the walking rebus of failure
    and cowardice, perihelion to the hot fist of correction,
marched to justice under the gonfalons of a love I'll spend
    the rest of my life trying to understand. Seven times
my father's hand turns my face, seven times he tells me
    what I am, what I will always be, because I am not
the son I should be. On the mantlepiece, a christmas flower drops
    petals as if from a balcony. A crust of slack slows the fire.

Melting figurines lean over the crib, and a faceless Virgin
    smokes blackly in the grate. Outside the window,
a colour-wheel of years whitens to the blizzard of '82. The roads
    are clogged with abandoned cars, and ice numbs the arterials
to estates where people slide and gimp the last leg home from work,
    happy in a friendly chaos. I work my shovel and know
the word for it: *sluasaid*; the word for soul: *anam*; the word for life: *saol*.
    My children watch me from a bedroom window, negotiating
foreign weather, clearing a path, restoring lost traction.
    I'll teach them little, make mistakes, and lose my way
for twenty years — when they sleep I trace their
    Irish names in frost.

Aporia

My unseen
finger tips

find new gaps

in the hair
of my crown.

How cold

and remote the skin of/to
an ageing touch.

Last Game Of The Night

It was precisely the wrong moment
I chanced to look through the skylight
to a cosmos where I was but a far-off
fish, my mind adrift. Pythagoras the puma
dealt the shiny new deck with a flick
of his wrist. Aquinas the hyena muttered
his usual *Tamquam Ignotums*, and Plato
the lion's prawn chilli sandwiches
did their ideal work, though the armagnac
was almost gone. I'd cleaned them out,
more or less, and the best of them,
Gödel the chimpanzee, had fifty at most.
The pot was replete but a long black shape
was ghosting the sky in that narrow
rectangle of night as I swigged
the last of the golden liquor, wiped
my fin, and cleared my scalded throat.
Then something came over me: I sang
like I never sang before, eight rattling bars
of an aria I'd heard at the Wexford opera.
Bravo! croaked Heisenberg the horned toad,
but Euclid the anaconda winked at Gödel,
and I knew I'd missed a trick when Pauli
the owl screeched a bibliopole scrunt
of delight and threw down a house
before shading the pot with his wings.
Then Riemann the croc dunted my ribs
with a claw, his maw a show of crushed
chillies and a skull that looked familiar,
his fat tongue lolling the skylight
where the glass had shattered and Dirac
the whale was fluking from the roof
to slip me an ace. It was '45 all over again:
Los Alamos, last game of the night, all-in,
with only me and Einstein the octopus

in the frame, the whole nine yards
in an inky pile and one card to go –
Trying to be nonchalant, I reprised the aria
with extra vibrato, but I was off-key
and my ballast popped when I spread
my flush with gusto, the table dropping
through oort clouds of boiling chilli breath
to an abyssal zone, a hadal depth where
nothing is proved, and all of us blown
through money and glass to a winter of stars.

Blood And Water

My cut hands blur in running water so cold
it's almost blue, like fire wrung out.
I wash the blebs off and ageless atoms sing
on my finger tips. Weeks of vaporous days wheel about

my sun-blinded eyes for a solid morning to hold on to,
and years at cross-purposes snib and hook
time, questioning in their daily fashion
the evidence of my life for a book

too opaque to read. I plead illiteracy -
I can't read the stone eyes of the bird in the yard,
or tell the constellation of a captured star
adrift in the rain barrel like a misplaced word.

But a younger self, older than me, answers for both of us —
Let me be a full-chambered gun, a sharpened scian.
Let me be transparent like the rain. Let me be more
than a war-beaten shield, holed by the sun's acetylene.

Corridors

With hindsight you can see all the way to the end
of the garden from the window where you stand
next to an empty bed, the vexed question
unanswerable now she's finally *home*.
She stared for hours at the trees, wanting to be
alone, but always needing company, and when
her look of constant surprise no longer
surprised, you watched terror float free
from the grip of her mind. *Nothing keeps*,
was the last intelligible thing she said,
and how right she was. The air in the room
was heavy with a fog only she could see,
now a clear window frames the garden
where flowers die back to a vegetable haze.
Down the long corridor someone drops a plate,
or throws one, the explosion is the same;
someone is complaining, or crying, or both –
And the way she looked through you to the trees
at the end of the garden – was it love or hate,
the mercurial heat that glazed the backs
of her eyes, the one true mirror of your life?

Stain

It's summer again
if you could call it that,

and the only certainty
is another day of rain

from a sky as dark
as the mind of a cat.

If God was listening
he'd tell you the stain

I work at night and day
has barely faded,

my one true original
by the old Master

no rain can wash away,
and my jaded scraping spins

my doldrums faster than any cyclone,
typhoon, or hurricane –

the great but little weather
of myself, baulked and stalled

to a micro climate of dull
and heavy air –

How late I was to find you,
wary of bright mornings,

in a squall mid-afternoon,
working a weather of your own

but somehow mine,
the door locked, the shutters down.

If You Do Not Come Too Close

Oblivious to the sap-cracked twig
and the dying grip of all that hardens,
the frost flowers suggest to him
nothing so much as frozen pringles.
No spirit exhales a blue uraeus above
his head, no ghost infuses the redbreast
blocking the path in the People's Gardens,
but his inward mind, never at rest,
gropes like a blind hand
through catacombs of memory
for a semblance of fire —
and when bird and breast combust,
as symbol and resurrection must,
he tastes the candent cup of loss
with the burnt-out tongue of pentecost.

The Fish

I was gutting fish and my hands were gloved
in scales. I held them to the light
and primed a momentary rainbow
from the shadeless bulb.

One hand gripped the colours and the other
worked the knife with a skill that was never mine.
When the skin of light was peeled away,
a woman looked at me from the flags.

She opened her arms, and I was naked,
already in her. She caressed me and I saw
the raw hulk of myself in her seal eyes.
I loved her with a lust that was never mine.

Her face, not young, was the face
of a woman I had loved. She turned,
and her body washed over me like a wave.
Scales fell across my eyes and I saw

old selves retreat in the rising spume.
The flags were hard and cold beneath us,
and when she stood me up
I knew her with an understanding

that was never mine. She laid me across
the boards and brought her face close,
her pupils now silver, now manganese.
Her low voice was the voice of the sea.

She whispered incantations she said
she'd learned from Poseidon himself.
Bright handfuls of scales fell over my face.
I responded in tongues that were never mine.

When she was finished, I was scaled
and simplified. She dropped me to the floor,
opened me from belly to neck, and slipped inside.
I slept for years, dreaming of fish

I would feed on with a hunger
that was never mine, and the sea,
how I found it, how I parted the air
with silver hands and walked into it.

Curtain Call

It all comes back: the pantry, the outhouse,
his hidden nook, pungent turps, Titbits,
an RIC man's helmet, salty books,
a gasmask, garden shears, a hoop,
torches, tins of soup, a folded tarp,
two skipping ropes, a brooch, sheets
for capes, draughts, a halloween mask,
a stuffed fox, kindling sticks, thumb tacks,
elastic bands, fingerless gloves, a bag of nails
like a face, hinges, marbles, a scunger, steelers,
pipes, rusty flanges, thermos flasks, locks, a belt,
broken hasps, discoloured jocks, his steel-toed boots,
unlaced shoes, sacks of unwashed clothes, two bishops,
copybooks, letters, brass scale weights, ballbearings, a rook,
odd socks, the last of his looks, a brush, a mop, a ten bob note,
pennys, florins, a magic plastic fish – every hard-up, hard-knocked
stoop-backed, hands-off, heart-stopping trick of sight – the blue light
turning the ceiling, the shimmering pleats like an eye spinning the dark.

Story

Not even Angkor Wat and Macchu Picchu
can compete with the latest loom
band craze: you've made a hundred
rainbow animals, each one more

intricate and beautiful than the last.
I take your cue and begin again:
pixies and stardust, friendly squirrels,
houses made from wheelie bins —

The story spins out over weeks
of school runs, elaborates and grows
like something woven. The pixies
and squirrels become your friends.

A week before the Easter break
I lose and can't find my bearings.
The story grows cold and hard as marble.
Nothing gives. I revert to pyramids

at Ghiza, the Sphinx, the Valley
of the Kings — a yarn about time-traveling
princesses and murderous clockwork beetles —
Start again, you say, pulling a thread

from the pig on your plastic loom.
I channel a town of woodland animals.
They live in bijou conversions made
from junk we pass along the way.

At the school gates I round off the episode,
small dangers hanging in the air.
And then, hood up, you're gone — in a downpour
that fizzles and clicks like a racing clepsydra —

Going the long way home, I finish the story for myself,
for the three-legged pig left behind. You and Nefertiti
are riot girls. And I am Michelangelo, perfecting
the stone that lets you go.

The Durable Note

Land and water are the first music,
the first poem. They shape the words
and notes, a singing god's one good trick.
From Glooria to Cloonshaghan the clouds
blend light and dark at the edge of summer.
Who speaks here speaks by tenets of weather.
When did I learn this small lake was ever,
and for all time, the unity of our number?
Mary Jo Casserly looked down at the water,
and said: 'Is it a he or a she, or what?'
as if the lake were a car or a boat.
And though it is neither, has no gender,
its breeze like a kiss will settle me down,
and a wave like a man's arm carry me home.

Sing body. Sing lake. Sing moon and tree.
None the wiser, I whistle into a sore distance
stronger than reason, whose eternities
are forevers so long as my breath holds. They dance
briefly to the tune. No music is mortal.
It flowers lifeless from the ground,
hides drumbeats in stones and water.
Hides gods in beetles and birds, in the sound
of their talk, their mutual silences.
The grasshopper stridulates the moon, catapults
hieroglyphs of sound over papyrus grasses
that will record nothing of this night's tumults.
What is it? Why dare listen for the ancient source,
distant, yet close, as my own incomprehensible force?

Whispers of waves and the news of waves.
Always the news, the same news of home.
Pillared realities capped by the mind's architraves.
The simple architecture I think of as my own.
Dark parts made of light, the union

of convenience that makes a place unique.
A family place whose embossed escutcheon
draws my tangle of keys to its lock.
Why call so frequently now? Why, when
no one is here in the home I called silence?
No gentle friend or cousin lives here. I lie down
under brute stars and outstare the violence
of my billion years of light to what simplifies,
the hungry complexity that feeds me to my eyes.

Out here on the low waves of Cavetown water,
the dead approach, their company no gift.
Tonight there's a metal echo of laughter
under angled sheets of tin, what's left
of an eight-hour summer on Ashford street.
We'd climbed spiked railings to a neighbour's
yard, built a gable cave from tyres and spars.
Candles lit, we powwowed on pinched sheets,
time-traveling. Now the drain pipe is ours to slide
down when the call comes in from the local P.D.
Someone hammers the roof. We rush the spikes.
Tommy Farren skewers himself above the knee.
Hanging upside down he burbles and snorts,
pale as a god, hoplite in bloody shorts.

The desert fathers went into the caves
of Egypt. Advanced far into themselves.
Until they found the retreat where gods live.
The withstood emptiness that trembled
stars and galaxies to consciousness.
Townland boys and girls are doing away
with themselves. Eyes locked on a darkness
to see by. Ingrown light of a day after a last day.
Turn over the ground. Plant a row of seeds.
Light a fire and prepare the meal.
If they speak at all this is what trees
and water say. This is their simplicity.
Yet I, who sucked on roots and drank a lake,
in my starving silence hear only a self speak.

On the day after the last day
I will not hear what angels say.
Or sing. Cast up from a burning floor
my soul won't melt the heavens' iron door.
Good and ill, I'll truck no more
in that war. I'll live, already dead,
in the unity of the primal host. For
that drop of blood my knowledge bled.
Knowing what I did not wish to know,
I do not ask to go, would rather stay,
and hazard to watch my invisibility grow
close and clear in a vanishing day,
a mist unstitched from a bed of reeds,
that opaque ghost who haunts my needs.

Closer and closer I came, to a breath
that was never mine, nor ever could be.
I felt its heat, and it warmed me
when I was coldest in my dearth
of home, and homeless was my name.
She took my name, and what I gave
her was not enough to close a claim
of distance that was other to me as love.
Now her being goes away from me in small
degrees, and her being, by being all
to me, longitudes separation, pulls east from west,
makes each a stranger that knows the other less.
And each is other by more than blood or name,
or round metaphor of miracle and signifying frame.

What changes is not the changes that I ring,
the loose whirls of time whiling away
from the oars. I go out on the water to sing
in a key that rivers inwardly. I've frayed
the perfect cloth I was born in, the one
I cast lots for with lifelong enemies.
And enemies will pass for friends. None
will be turned away. Let Caesars and Ptolemies
dress in fineries gold as the sun.

I'll meet them head on with little bitterness.
I'll meet and defend them from their lone
accuser, myself, until that bitter littleness
sees itself in the lake's eye grown moon blind
in rags, and hears the tune that plays a mind.

I will learn that tune by an impossible learning.
And the lesson is my life, which is not mine
to own. I foreclose a tenanted yearning
to discover that distinction, always fine,
the ideal of itself in the renters note I whistle
over the low waves of Cavetown lake.
A forefather's melody of bone and muscle.
The seed breath in the trees, the lungfuls I take
as droplets fall from the oars
in the dark, fall as diamonds into a black sun.
I will dissolve with them, with this night for
rowing, into the dreaming atoms of the tune.
My inheritance will be that first and only melody,
before the first word, the first and only body.

I lie athwart, allow the boat to drift.
Above me the dark I lay out will lift
small stars into my eyes as patterns.
I'll not remember them. My scattered
thoughts will not desert me when peace
mortars down oblivions of waking sleep.
Here on the night waters I whistle wrong
shapes into form, dream my life in a song
I never wrote and yet has written me.
It sings through my pores its durable notes.
They fife my living bones with the litany
of sighs I make with rib and throat.
Around the lake my wife's returning car
lights the water, dims the moon and stars.

A sweeping curve, here and not there.
Is it real? The sound of the oars is real.
The car engine dies on a last bend of air.

The water gives the oars their wooden feel.
What shafts my arms to a cold look
that sees in the dark, the small arcs
repeating like bits of clockwork?
What powers my mind to torque
this rough flatness into distance?
I'm tiring. The far bank grows clear.
Michael Casserly's unfinished house
hunkers out like a crab to the shore.
The windows pale in planktons of dark.
Mayfly negatives pair up around my ark.

Pulling dumbly, I draw hard and work
my thoughts through instants of diachrony
to no conclusion. History will not truck
with me. Transparently, before and after me,
water evolves the wake I speak as no trace.
The light denies dark oncoming battlefields
where common agonies must be faced.
And the dark denies the light that shields
its unknowable source. I'll close my eyes,
have it both ways. I'll find the tune again.
Under my eyelids are notes of ground and sky,
the wet proximates of hell and heaven.
A melody goes over and under me.
I am its element and poverty.

Crossing The Jade River
After Meeting A Friend

Leave the gods to their eternal spring,
speaking animals to the story hearth.
Better to believe in your own breath,
poem of everything and nothing.

You will forget me — this is destiny.
On your journey without turnings,
you won't remember me,
or the torn silk I wrote this on.

Notes

Page 24 — *"For Living Things Are Revived By Food, And Clocks, By Lapse Of Time, Become Slower, Never Faster"*

Giovanni Di Dondi (1318-1389), professor of astronomy, logic and medicine at Padua University, in a treatise on his astronomical clock (built 1348-1364), provides the first manuscript diagram of a clock escapement: a crownwheel and verge. The first known description of a foliot is given in a poem (La Orloge Amoreuse) by Jean Froissart, in 1369. Foliot derives from Follet, a french word, meaning one who dances about madly. Spring driven clocks were invented for domestic use. The spring, made of hammered brass, did not provide a constant source of power, unlike falling weight clocks. Because the middle range of power was the most useful, force reduction was a major problem. Springs also suffered from clustering, as they were not evenly made and didn't coil accurately. The first step to the solution of these problems was to limit spring action to the middle range by using a brake known as a stackfreed, and secondly, to even out power output with a gearing mechanism (fusee). The earliest known diagram of a fusee is from a document (1450-1460) in the Royal Library in Brussels. The first printed book, (Basle, 1557) illustrated with clock movements, including a fusee, is one of series of books written by Jerome Cardan, who added a note about the spring (damp, rust, dust, etc.). The fusee itself was probably developed from similar devices used in ancient war machines.

Page 27 — *"Cranmer And The Yellow Flower"*

Henry VIII, Act V, Scene II, William Shakespeare.
In The Storm of Roses, Ingeborg Bachman.

Page 37 – *"Petronilla De Meath"*

Petronilla De Meath was burned at the stake in Kilkenny on the 3rd of November 1324, the first known case of burning at the stake in Ireland or Great Britain for heresy.

Page 43 – *"If A Lion Could Talk"*

Philosophical Investigations, Ludwig Wittgenstein.

Page 58 – *"Vrelo Bosne"*

Vrelo Bosne is the spring of the river Bosna, Sarajevo, Bosnia and Herzegovina.

Page 60 – *"Meiteamorfóis"*

Siúcra, subh, im : Sugar, jam, butter
As Béarla! : In English!

JOHN MURPHY lives and works in Dublin. He was shortlisted three times for the Hennessy/Sunday Tribune New Irish Writing prize. His debut collection, *The Book of Water* was published by Salmon in 2012, and was well received. He has been shortlisted four times for the Bridport Prize (prizewinner, 2013), and specially commended in the Patrick Kavanagh Award. He won the Strokestown International Poetry Prize in 2015. In 2016, he was a finalist in UK National Poetry Competition. He won the Strokestown International Poetry Prize for a second time in 2016. He was educated at Trinity College where he received his Ph.D in 1994. He has worked as a computer scientist in industry (IBM) and in academia (DCU) for more than thirty years.